Gender and Sexual Assault.

Examining the Role Gender plays in Sexual Assault

Flawless Dave

Table of Contents

Introduction

Today, we are beginning a journey to learn more about gender-based violence and sexual assault.

Gender-based violence and sexual assault are serious issues that affect people all over the world, regardless of age, gender, or culture. These acts of violence are a violation of human rights and go against the principles of equality, safety, and dignity. By understanding the complexity of these issues, we can work towards preventing and addressing them effectively.

It is our hope that one day everyone will feel safe, respected, and free from violence. Unfortunately, we are still far from achieving this goal. Gender-based violence can take many forms, such as domestic violence, sexual harassment, intimate partner violence, and forced marriage. These acts of violence are often rooted in gender inequality, harmful gender norms, and power imbalances.

Let's consider an example. Meet Sarah, a young woman who has experienced sexual harassment in her workplace. Despite her talents and hard work, she is constantly subjected to unwelcome advances and inappropriate comments from her supervisor. This not only affects her mental well-being but also hinders her professional growth. Sarah's experience is just one of many instances where gender-based violence is present in everyday life, preventing individuals from achieving their goals and living a happy life.

The effects of gender-based violence go beyond the immediate victims. It can have a ripple effect on families, communities, and societies, creating a climate of fear, trauma, and inequality. This makes it clear that addressing gender-based violence is not just an individual responsibility but a collective effort that requires social change, awareness, and action.

Throughout our discussions, we will look at various aspects related to gender-based violence and sexual assault. We will examine the role of gender in these issues, analyzing the influence of societal expectations, power dynamics, and victimization. We will also discuss the importance of support services, gender-inclusive policies, education, and awareness in preventing and combating gender-based violence.

Together, we will explore this complex topic, seeking understanding, sharing insights, and empowering ourselves to contribute to a more equitable and violence-free world. Through engaging conversations, informative examples, and a commitment to change, we can make a difference in the lives of individuals impacted by gender-based violence and sexual assault.

So, let's start this enlightening journey, ready to challenge assumptions, broaden our perspectives, and take meaningful action. By the end of our exploration, you will have gained valuable insights, resources, and a deeper understanding of gender-based violence and sexual assault.

Chapter 1: Understanding Gender and Sexual Assault

Defining Gender

Let's start by discussing gender and its complexities. Gender is a multifaceted part of our identity, which includes a range of characteristics, roles, behaviors, and expectations that society assigns to people based on their perceived sex. While sex is related to biological factors, such as reproductive organs and chromosomes, gender goes beyond these. It is important to note that gender is not only determined by one's biological sex. It is a social construct that varies across cultures and changes over time.

Traditionally, people have been classified as either male or female based on their biological sex. However, this binary view of gender is limited because it does not take into account the wide range of human experiences. Nowadays, many people recognize that gender is not confined to a two-category system. We understand that gender exists on a spectrum, encompassing a variety of identities and expressions. For instance, someone may identify as male, female, both, neither, or something else entirely. These diverse gender identities include transgender, non-binary, genderqueer, genderfluid, and many more.

To illustrate this point further, let's consider two examples. Alex was assigned female at birth, but they identify as non-binary, meaning they don't exclusively identify as male or female. Alex prefers to use they/them pronouns. This example shows that gender identity is not necessarily tied to the sex assigned at birth. On the other hand, Taylor was assigned male at birth and identifies as a woman. She has undergone a transition and uses she/her pronouns. This case highlights that gender identity is deeply personal and may differ from societal expectations.

It is essential to understand and respect diverse gender identities in order to create an inclusive and supportive society. We should use the correct pronouns and address individuals by their self-identified gender. This way, we show respect for their identity and contribute to a more accepting environment.

Now, let's briefly talk about gender and its connection to sexual assault. Sexual assault is a serious issue that affects people of all genders. It is important to remember that sexual assault is not about the gender identity of the survivor, but about the violation of consent and boundaries. It can happen to anyone, regardless of their gender identity. It is a form of violence that includes non-consensual sexual acts, harassment, or any unwanted sexual advances. No one ever asks for or deserves to experience sexual assault, regardless of their gender or any other factor.

In order to create a safe and supportive environment for survivors of sexual assault, we must actively challenge harmful gender stereotypes and promote consent education. By understanding and respecting diverse gender identities, we can contribute to a culture that values consent, empowers survivors, and works towards preventing sexual assault.

Defining Sexual Assault

Sexual assault is a very serious issue that affects people of all genders. It is any form of sexual activity or behavior that is done without the explicit consent of the person involved. It is important to remember that the survivor is never to blame for the assault and that it is a violation of their autonomy and boundaries.

To better understand this concept, let's look at a couple of examples. Sarah is a college student who is at a party with her friends. She meets an acquaintance named Mark and they start talking. Without Sarah's permission, Mark begins to touch her inappropriately. Sarah tries to express her discomfort but Mark ignores her. In this situation, Mark's actions are considered sexual assault because he engaged in sexual behavior without Sarah's consent.

Another example is Chris, a transgender person who identifies as male. He is at a bar and meets a stranger named Alex. As the night goes on, Alex becomes more aggressive and tries to force Chris into sexual activity, disregarding his lack of consent. This shows that sexual assault can happen to people of any gender identity, emphasizing the importance of understanding that everyone is vulnerable to this type of violence.

It is essential to remember that consent is a key part of any sexual activity. It must be given freely, without any form of manipulation, coercion, or pressure. Consent can be withdrawn at any time and it is never assumed or implied. It is important to understand that a lack of resistance or silence does not mean consent.

Sexual assault is a serious violation of an individual's bodily autonomy and personal boundaries. Survivors may experience a range of emotional and physical effects, such as trauma, fear, depression, anxiety, and physical injuries. It is important to provide support, understanding, and resources to survivors, encouraging them to seek help and access the necessary medical and emotional support.

Preventing sexual assault requires a collective effort from society. This includes challenging gender norms and stereotypes, educating people about consent, and creating safe spaces where survivors feel comfortable coming forward and getting help.

The Role of Gender in Sexual Assault

Gender plays a major role in influencing the dynamics and experiences of sexual assault. By understanding this role, we can gain valuable insights into the complexities of this issue.

It is important to recognize that sexual assault can happen to people of any gender, and perpetrators can also be of any gender. It is a misconception to think that sexual assault is only a crime committed by men against women. Acknowledging the diversity of survivors and perpetrators is essential for understanding and addressing sexual assault effectively.

Let's look at a couple of examples to illustrate the role of gender in sexual assault. Imagine a situation where Alex, a male college student, attends a party. He meets a female acquaintance named Lisa, who has been drinking heavily. Lisa takes advantage of Alex's intoxicated state and engages in non-consensual sexual activity with him. In this case, Lisa, a woman, is the perpetrator of sexual assault against Alex, a man. This example challenges the stereotypical notion that only men can be perpetrators and shows that anyone can commit sexual assault, regardless of their gender.

Another example involves Sarah, a woman who works in an office environment. Her supervisor, David, consistently makes unwanted sexual advances towards her, creates a hostile work environment, and threatens her with professional consequences if she doesn't comply. In this case, Sarah experiences sexual harassment, which is a form of sexual assault, perpetrated by David, a man. This example highlights that sexual assault can occur in various contexts, including the workplace, and emphasizes the importance of addressing power imbalances and creating safe environments for all individuals.

Gender norms, stereotypes, and power dynamics in society can contribute to sexual assault. Traditional ideas of masculinity and femininity often perpetuate harmful beliefs and attitudes that can lead to the objectification, harassment, or assault of individuals. For instance, rigid expectations of male dominance and entitlement can fuel acts of sexual violence. Similarly, societal pressures that ignore or dismiss the experiences of male survivors can create obstacles for seeking help and support.

Chapter 2: Gender Roles and Sexual Assault

Gender Roles and Socialization

Gender roles are the societal expectations, norms, and behaviors associated with masculinity and femininity. These roles are learned and reinforced through a process called socialization, which starts early and continues throughout our lives. Examining the influence of gender roles and socialization can help us understand the dynamics of sexual assault.

From a young age, society often assigns specific roles and expectations based on an individual's perceived gender. For instance, boys are expected to be tough, assertive, and dominant, while girls are expected to be caring, passive, and submissive. These gender roles can shape our attitudes, behaviors, and interactions, often leading to harmful power dynamics and contributing to the prevalence of sexual assault.

Let's consider a few examples to illustrate the impact of gender roles and socialization. Imagine two siblings, Alex and Sam. Alex, assigned male at birth, is told by their parents to "man up" and not show emotions. On the other hand, Sam, assigned female at birth, is taught to be accommodating and put others' needs before her own. These gender role expectations can limit their ability to express themselves fully and may also affect their understanding of consent and boundaries.

Now, let's imagine a different scenario. Claire, a young girl, is given dolls and taught domestic skills, while her brother, James, is given toy cars and encouraged to engage in physical activities. These gender-specific toys and activities reinforce traditional gender roles and limit the range of experiences and skills children develop. These rigid gender roles can contribute to unequal power dynamics and create environments where sexual assault is more likely to occur.

It's important to note that gender roles and socialization are not necessarily bad. They can provide guidance and structure for individuals, but when they become too restrictive and oppressive, they can perpetuate harmful stereotypes and contribute to a culture that tolerates or ignores sexual assault.

Challenging and reshaping gender roles and socialization is essential in preventing sexual assault. By promoting gender equality and encouraging individuals of all genders to express themselves freely, we can create a society where consent, respect, and healthy relationships thrive.

Education is key to challenging harmful gender roles. By teaching young people about consent, boundaries, and healthy relationships, we can empower them to challenge oppressive norms and foster a culture of respect and equality. Breaking down gender stereotypes and allowing individuals to explore their identities without judgement can also contribute to creating a more inclusive society.

Gender Roles and Power Dynamics

Gender roles can often lead to power imbalances based on societal expectations of masculinity and femininity. Generally, men are seen as dominant, assertive, and in control, while women are expected to be passive, submissive, and accommodating. This power dynamic can create an environment where sexual assault is more likely to occur, as the power imbalance can be taken advantage of and consent disregarded.

To illustrate this connection, let's look at a couple of examples. Take a workplace scenario where John, a male supervisor, is making inappropriate comments and advances towards his female subordinate, Sarah. John's position of authority gives him power over Sarah, making it difficult for her to resist or report his behavior. In this case, gender roles and power dynamics intersect, creating a situation where sexual harassment and assault may occur.

Another example is the societal expectation that men should always be sexually assertive. This can lead to situations where consent is not taken into account and boundaries are crossed. For instance, Mike is on a date with Lisa. Due to societal pressure to conform to traditional gender roles, Mike feels compelled to initiate sexual activity without explicitly obtaining Lisa's consent or checking her comfort level. Here, the influence of gender roles and power dynamics can undermine the importance of enthusiastic and ongoing consent.

It's important to remember that power dynamics can exist within any gender pairing. While traditional gender roles often depict men as perpetrators and women as victims, individuals of any gender can be both survivors and perpetrators of sexual assault. Acknowledging this complexity is essential in providing support to all survivors and holding all perpetrators accountable, regardless of gender.

Gender Roles and Victimization

Gender roles can have a detrimental effect on individuals, particularly when they reinforce damaging stereotypes and expectations. It is important to understand this connection in order to comprehend the impact of gender roles on sexual assault.

Women are often seen as more vulnerable and men as more powerful and aggressive due to societal expectations. This can create an atmosphere where women are viewed as "easy targets" and their experiences of sexual assault may be disregarded or trivialized. Additionally, rigid gender roles may discourage men from coming forward as survivors, as they may feel that their experiences will not be taken seriously due to the expectation of strength and invulnerability.

To illustrate the link between gender roles and victimization, let's consider a few examples. For instance, a woman named Emily walking home alone at night may feel a heightened sense of fear and vulnerability due to traditional gender roles that depict women as weaker and more prone to harm. This fear is intensified by societal narratives that place the responsibility for safety on women, rather than addressing the root causes of sexual violence.

Another example involves a man named Tom, who experiences sexual assault by a female acquaintance. Due to societal expectations that men should always be sexually eager and assertive, Tom may face difficulties in acknowledging his experience and seeking help. The influence of gender roles can create obstacles for men to come forward as survivors, as their experiences may be met with doubt or disbelief.

It is essential to recognize that anyone, regardless of gender, can be a victim of sexual assault. By perpetuating the idea that certain genders are more likely to be victimized, we not only propagate harmful stereotypes but also impede the healing and support process for survivors.

Breaking away from harmful gender roles and challenging victim-blaming narratives is essential in preventing sexual assault. This involves creating a culture where victim blaming is not tolerated, survivors are supported, and the responsibility for preventing sexual violence is placed on the perpetrators rather than the victims. Additionally, fostering an environment of consent education, empathy, and respect can contribute to a society where survivors feel empowered to seek assistance and support.

Chapter 3: Gender-Based Violence and Sexual Assault

Gender-Based Violence

Gender-based violence is a serious issue that is rooted in power imbalances and gender norms. It can take many forms, such as sexual assault, domestic violence, harassment, and other forms of violence that disproportionately affect individuals because of their gender. It is important to note that both men and women can be victims of gender-based violence, although women and girls tend to be disproportionately affected.

Let's look at a few examples to better understand gender-based violence. For instance, consider a woman named Maya who is in an abusive relationship with her partner, Jake. Jake exhibits controlling behavior, physically assaults Maya, and undermines her autonomy. This is an example of gender-based violence, as it reflects a pattern of harmful behavior driven by power imbalances and societal expectations of male dominance.

Another example is workplace harassment. Emma, a woman working in a male-dominated industry, faces persistent sexist comments, unwanted advances, and exclusion from professional opportunities. This type of gender-based violence creates a hostile work environment and restricts Emma's ability to thrive professionally.

Gender-based violence can occur in different settings and be perpetrated by individuals known to the survivor, such as intimate partners or family members, or by strangers in public spaces. To address this issue, we must challenge the societal norms that perpetuate harmful gender stereotypes, promote gender equality, and advocate for policies and programs that support survivors and hold perpetrators accountable. By fostering a culture of respect, consent, and empowerment, we can work towards eliminating gender-based violence and creating safer environments for all.

Gender-Based Violence and Sexual Assault

Gender-based violence is any form of violence or harmful behavior that is mainly directed at people based on their gender, while sexual assault is when someone is forced to engage in sexual acts without their consent. It is important to understand the connection between these two concepts to comprehend the complexities of violence against individuals based on their gender.

Gender-based violence includes sexual assault, domestic violence, female genital mutilation, forced marriage, and more. These acts are caused by power imbalances, gender norms, and the need to control others. Although gender-based violence affects people of all genders, women and girls are more likely to be affected.

Let's look at sexual assault as a form of gender-based violence with a few examples. For instance, Sarah is walking home alone at night and is attacked by a stranger who sexually assaults her. This act of sexual violence shows the intersection of gender-based violence and sexual assault, as Sarah's vulnerability and victimization are linked to her gender.

Another example is intimate partner violence. Chris and Alex are in a same-sex relationship. Chris, who is controlling and abusive, sexually assaults Alex. In this case, the sexual assault is a form of gender-based violence, as it occurs in an intimate relationship and reflects an abuse of power.

It is important to note that sexual assault can happen in various settings, with people known to the survivor or strangers. No matter the circumstances, sexual assault is a violation of a person's bodily autonomy and consent, leaving long-term physical, emotional, and psychological effects.

To address gender-based violence and sexual assault, we need to take comprehensive steps. This includes raising awareness, challenging gender norms and power imbalances, teaching consent, providing support and resources to survivors, and holding perpetrators accountable. By creating a culture of respect, consent, and gender equality, we can work towards preventing and addressing gender-based violence and sexual assault.

Gender-Based Violence and the Law

Laws are an essential part of the fight against gender-based violence, providing a framework for prevention, protection, and justice. It is important to understand the relationship between gender-based violence and the law in order to comprehend how legal systems can help address this pervasive issue.

The laws related to gender-based violence vary from country to country, but many have legislation specifically designed to address violence against individuals based on their gender. These laws cover a wide range of topics, such as sexual assault, domestic violence, stalking, and harassment, and they define these acts as criminal offenses with penalties for perpetrators.

For instance, a law criminalizing marital rape acknowledges the importance of consent in intimate relationships and gives survivors legal recourse and protection. Similarly, protection orders for victims of domestic violence provide survivors with legal mechanisms to seek safety and keep their abusers away. By having the law on their side, survivors are empowered to take the necessary steps to protect themselves and seek justice.

Laws related to sexual assault also focus on ensuring consent, defining the parameters of consent, and making it clear that non-consensual sexual acts are criminal offenses. These laws shift the burden of responsibility onto the perpetrators, emphasizing the importance of consent and establishing clear boundaries.

However, laws alone are not enough to combat gender-based violence. Implementation, enforcement, and accessibility of legal frameworks are key challenges. In many cases, survivors face obstacles such as stigma, lack of resources, fear of retaliation, or bias within the legal system, which can hinder their access to justice.

Therefore, addressing gender-based violence through the law requires ongoing efforts. This includes raising awareness about existing legislation, advocating for policy reforms, and ensuring that legal frameworks are victim-centered, culturally sensitive, and responsive to the needs of all survivors. This also involves providing support services, legal aid, and specialized training for law enforcement and judicial officials.

By striving to create comprehensive legal frameworks and their effective implementation, we can work towards a society where gender-based violence is not tolerated and survivors are supported in their journey towards healing and justice.

Chapter 4: Gender and Sexual Assault Prevention

Education and Awareness

Education is a key factor in combating negative attitudes, promoting consent, and giving individuals the power to be active players in creating a safer and more inclusive society. By understanding the importance of education and awareness, we can make a real contribution to preventing gender-based violence.

Education and awareness initiatives are designed to tackle the root causes of gender-based violence by challenging social norms, stereotypes, and power imbalances. They provide people with knowledge about healthy relationships, consent, and the importance of respect and equality. These initiatives can take many forms, such as school-based programs, community workshops, online campaigns, and public awareness campaigns.

To better understand the importance of education and awareness, let's look at a few examples. Think of a high school that has a comprehensive sexual education curriculum that goes beyond the biological aspects and includes discussions on consent, healthy relationships, and boundaries. By giving students accurate information and encouraging open dialogue, this curriculum equips them with the tools to understand and navigate relationships in a respectful and consensual way, helping to prevent sexual assault.

Another example is public awareness campaigns that challenge victim-blaming narratives and promote bystander intervention. These campaigns urge people to take action when they witness potentially harmful situations and provide resources for reporting and supporting survivors. By promoting a culture of responsibility and empathy, these initiatives empower communities to work together to prevent and address gender-based violence.

It is essential to recognize that education and awareness should be ongoing and target people of all ages. By starting conversations early, we can instill healthy attitudes and behaviors from childhood, laying the groundwork for respectful relationships. This includes teaching children about consent, boundaries, and gender equality, creating a society that values and respects the rights and autonomy of all individuals.

Moreover, education and awareness must be inclusive and intersectional, recognizing that gender-based violence affects people of all genders, races, ethnicities, sexual orientations, and socioeconomic backgrounds. By addressing the unique challenges faced by different communities, we can make sure that prevention efforts are effective and reach those who are most vulnerable.

By prioritizing education and awareness, we can create a culture that rejects gender-based violence and supports survivors. This requires collaboration between schools, communities, and government agencies, as well as the active participation of parents, teachers, and individuals.

Gender-Inclusive Policies

Gender-inclusive policies are like a superhero team, ready to swoop in and save the day! They work to promote gender equality, break down harmful stereotypes, and create safe and inclusive environments for everyone. Understanding the importance of these policies can help us actively work to prevent gender-based violence.

Gender-inclusive policies are all about equal rights and opportunities for all genders. They cover a range of areas, such as education, workplaces, public spaces, and healthcare. Their mission is to challenge gender norms, eliminate discrimination, and create supportive environments where everyone can thrive.

Let's look at a few examples. A university might have a policy on sexual harassment and assault that ensures reports are taken seriously, provides support services for survivors, and holds perpetrators accountable. This sends a strong message that gender-based violence won't be tolerated and survivors will be heard.

Workplaces can also have policies that promote gender equality and prevent harassment and discrimination. These might include anti-sexual harassment training, gender-neutral dress codes, equal pay provisions, and flexible work arrangements. By creating respectful and inclusive work environments, these policies can help prevent gender-based violence.

Gender-inclusive policies should also consider the needs and experiences of marginalized groups, such as transgender and non-binary individuals, immigrants, and individuals with disabilities. These policies should be intersectional, addressing the unique challenges faced by different communities and making sure everyone is included.

Gender-inclusive policies don't just apply to formal institutions. They can also be implemented at the community level. For instance, public spaces can have policies that prioritize safety, such as well-lit areas, accessible public transportation, and gender-neutral restroom facilities. These measures create environments where people feel secure and respected, reducing the risk of gender-based violence.

Gender-inclusive policies are essential for challenging gender stereotypes, dismantling systems of oppression, and creating inclusive spaces that prioritize the well-being and safety of all individuals. But policies alone aren't enough.

We need education, awareness, and a collective commitment to creating cultural change.

Advocating for gender-inclusive policies is a team effort that involves community organizations, activists, policymakers, and all of us. By supporting and championing policies that promote gender equality and prevent gender-based violence, we can help build a society that respects and protects the rights and dignity of everyone.

Support Services

Support services are essential in providing assistance, resources, and care to those who have experienced gender-based violence. By recognizing the importance of these services, we can work together to create a safe and supportive environment for survivors.

Support services encompass a wide range of resources tailored to meet the individual needs of survivors. This can include helplines, counseling services, medical support, legal aid, and shelters. These services are designed to address the short-term and long-term effects of gender-based violence, offering survivors a path to healing, recovery, and empowerment.

To better understand the impact of support services, let's look at a few examples. Take Maya, a survivor of sexual assault. She reaches out to a helpline specifically dedicated to supporting survivors of gender-based violence. The professionals on the helpline provide her with emotional support, inform her of available resources, and guide her through the next steps, such as reporting the assault or seeking medical attention. This helpline becomes a lifeline for Maya, offering her a listening ear and connecting her to the help she needs.

Another example is counseling services provided by specialized organizations. Survivors can access individual or group counseling, which helps them process their trauma, develop coping mechanisms, and rebuild their lives. These services create a safe space where survivors can share their experiences, receive validation, and receive professional guidance on their journey to healing.

Support services also extend to legal aid, ensuring that survivors have access to information and assistance in navigating the legal system. Legal professionals can help survivors understand their rights, provide guidance on reporting incidents, and support them through court proceedings. This assistance is essential in empowering survivors to seek justice and hold perpetrators accountable.

Furthermore, support services may include safe shelters or housing options for individuals who need a secure and supportive environment to escape violence. These shelters provide survivors with temporary accommodation, basic necessities, and access to various support services. They offer a refuge where survivors can rebuild their lives free from the threat of further violence.

It's important to note that support services should be accessible, inclusive, and culturally sensitive. They should be tailored to the unique needs of individuals from different backgrounds, including survivors from marginalized communities. Organizations providing support services should be well-funded and have trained staff who understand the specific challenges faced by survivors of gender-based violence.

Conclusion

Throughout this voyage, we have investigated a variety of angles of this significant subject, from understanding gender roles and power dynamics to inspecting support services and gender-inclusive policies. Presently, let us think back on what we have realized and examine the significance of taking action.

Gender-based violence and sexual assault are pervasive issues that influence individuals of all genders, ages, races, and backgrounds. They stem from profound established social inequalities, hurtful gender standards, and power imbalances. Be that as it may, by teaching ourselves, raising awareness, and actively working towards change, we can have any kind of effect.

We have realized that understanding gender roles and socialization assists us with recognizing how social desires and generalizations can add to a culture that keeps up violence. By testing these standards and advancing regard, assent, and equality, we can work towards forestalling gender-based violence.

Examining power dynamics has thrown light on how power imbalances can empower and keep up acts of violence. By tending to these power dynamics and supporting for frameworks that advance fairness, equity, and responsibility, we can make situations where gender-based violence is less inclined to happen.

We have additionally talked about the job of support services in giving help and assets to survivors. By supporting and supporting for available, well-funded, and socially delicate support services, we can guarantee that survivors have the important instruments and care to mend and reconstruct their lives.

Moreover, we investigated the significance of gender-inclusive policies that advance equality and secure individuals from violence and segregation. By supporting these policies and supporting for their usage, we add to making situations that are protected, comprehensive, and respectful for all.

Education and awareness rose as incredible instruments in anticipation. By testing hurtful perspectives, advancing assent, and supporting open exchange, we can work towards a society that esteems and regards the privileges and freedom of all individuals.

Lastly, we perceived that tending to gender-based violence requires a collective effort. It requires collaboration between individuals, networks, associations, and policymakers. By remaining together, we can make a culture that dismisses violence and supports survivors.

As we finish up, I urge you to stay informed, take an interest in conversations, and take action in your own capacity. Every one of us has a job to carry out in forestalling gender-based violence and making a more secure and progressively equitable world. Whether it's supporting survivors, supporting for change, or testing hurtful perspectives, your voice and activities matter.

Let us keep on learning, developing, and working towards a future where gender-based violence and sexual assault are never again endured, and all individuals can live their lives liberated from dread and violence. Together, we can have any kind of effect.